Other Books Available at Holloway.com

The Holloway Guide to Remote Work
Katie Womersley, Juan Pablo Buriticá et al.

A comprehensive guide to building, managing, and adapting to working with distributed teams.

The Holloway Guide to Technical Recruiting and Hiring
Osman (Ozzie) Osman et al.

A practical, expert-reviewed guide to growing software engineering teams effectively, written by and for hiring managers, recruiters, interviewers, and candidates.

The Holloway Guide to Equity Compensation
Joshua Levy, Joe Wallin et al.

Stock options, RSUs, job offers, and taxes—a detailed reference, explained from the ground up.

The Holloway Guide to Raising Venture Capital
Andy Sparks et al.

A current and comprehensive resource for entrepreneurs, with technical detail, practical knowledge, real-world scenarios, and pitfalls to avoid.

Founding Sales: The Early-Stage Go-To-Market Handbook
Pete Kazanjy

This tactical handbook distills early sales first principles, and teaches the skills required for going from being a founder to early salesperson, and eventually becoming an early sales leader.

Angel Investing: Start to Finish
Joe Wallin, Pete Baltaxe

A journey through the perils and rewards of angel investing, from fundamentals to finding deals, financings, and term sheets.

Art For Money

Art For Money

UP YOUR FREELANCE GAME AND GET PAID WHAT YOU'RE WORTH

Michael Ardelean

A collection of personal and practical advice for creative freelancers on winning clients and getting paid for their work.

RACHEL JEPSEN, EDITOR

HOLLOWAY

Published in the United States by Holloway, San Francisco
Holloway.com

Cover design by Order (New York) and Andy Sparks
Interior design by Joshua Levy and Jennifer Durrant
Print engineering by Titus Wormer

Typefaces: Tiempos Text and National 2
by Kris Sowersby of Klim Type Foundry

Print version 1.0 · Digital version e1.0.0
doc 13b82a · pipeline d2b39a · genbook 83632a
2021-02-10

A Note from the Publisher

Holloway publishes books online. As a reader of this special full-access print edition, you are granted personal access to the paid digital edition, which you can read and share on the web, and offers commentary, updates, and corrections. A Holloway account also gives access to search, definitions of key terms, bookmarks, highlights, and other features. Claim your account by visiting: **holloway.com/print20350**

If you wish to recommend the book to others, suggest they visit **holloway.com/afm** to learn more and purchase their own digital or print copy.

The author welcomes your feedback! Please consider adding comments or suggestions to the book online so others can benefit. Or say hello@holloway.com. Thank you for reading.

The Holloway team

LEGEND

Some elements in the text are marked for special significance:

| ◇ **IMPORTANT** | Important or often overlooked tip |
| ◇ **CAUTION** | Caution, limitation, or problem |

Web links appear as numbered footnotes in print.

References to other related sections are indicated by superscript section numbers, prefixed with §.

TABLE OF CONTENTS

1 Foreword

I first met Mike a couple years ago at a coffee shop in LA, when my husband and I sat down for a cortado with him and his wife. Mike, a former Pro BMX colleague of my husband's, struck me as the quiet type—pensive with a propensity for listening. His remarks were measured. When he spoke, we listened. It wasn't just what he said that intrigued me, it was the affirmation in which he said it.

Over time, our mutual affinities and beliefs sparked a series of conversations.

We connected through social media and discussed creative ideas, future business goals, and matters orbiting life itself. Mike would present his opinions with the tenacious confidence of someone who had experienced many facets of business, and learned diligently from them. I'd gravitate towards his words, then I'd walk away with a perspective that would soon become my own.

As a Creative Director, agency founder, and influencer, I was wading through the murky waters of freelance contracts and expectations. To put it simply: I was having a difficult time pricing my worth, creating healthy relationships, and establishing a business structure that supported me.

I reached out to Mike for help, knowing he'd built several ventures across multiple creative mediums, and he said "hold tight." Then he sent over the book you're about to read.

After that, my income tripled. My self-worth skyrocketed. And my clients respected my role as a creative with the same fervor that I poured into my craft.

This book became my North Star.

So, to the other creatives who look to the stars, to the writer, the graphic designer, agency owner, software builder, entrepreneur, painter, musician, storyboarder—Mike wrote this book for you.

In the pages that follow, he shows you how to respect your business with the same passion you use to create; to build boundaries that set the framework for mutually beneficial relationships; to organize your business structure for profitability; to ensure every client respects your time.

He shows you how to make your art and get your money.

As creative entrepreneurs, we don't create to make money. We nurture our art because there is simply nothing else we'd ever do. Period. Through Mike's storied experiences and successes, he reshapes the narrative of the Freelancer, putting us in the driver's seat.

Instead of a 300-page manifesto on how to dominate the freelance market, he breaks down certain phenomena at the human level, addressing the psyche on both sides (client and freelancer) and presenting his information in under 80 pages of no-bullshit action items.

Through this short and entertaining lecture, I found my moral compass in the Wild West of freelance business. This book offered me perspective by answering questions like:

What do I need from my clients? What do they need from me? Where are those needs misaligned and how do I, in a professional manner, ensure they run parallel prior to diving into a project I haven't yet been paid for?

At the end of the day, this guide isn't just a commentary; it's a toolkit that helps you actualize the solutions Mike presents. One that's applicable to creatives and freelancers alike.

So, if you're ready to reclaim agency of your craft and start making more money (and sleeping eight hours a night), then it's time to turn the page.

— Angela Fink

@angelafink on Instagram[1]

---

1. https://www.instagram.com/angelafink/

2 Dedication

"Art is a gift that changes the recipient."

— Seth Godin

To my friends, whose work is very valuable.

And to...

illustrators, graphic designers, copy writers, web developers, software engineers, craftspeople, builders, landscape architects, furniture designers, photographers, videographers, editors, automotive detailers, ceramicists, cake artists, florists, painters, mural artists, coaches, instructors, models, influencers, hair and makeup artists, producers, directors, consultants, journalists, content creators, project managers, contract workers

...and independent creators of all kinds.

3 My Mess Is My Message

"Getting results doesn't take much time at all. It's not getting
results that takes up all the time."

— Dan Sullivan

A while back, after a career in fashion merchandising and alongside my freelance pursuits, I became a partner in a small product design studio. My title was Managing Director. My partners did the design work and I ran the business.

All seemed to be going well until we brought on board a client who, after a few months, stopped paying their bills and started acting weird. Communication came in a tangled web and decisions were stalled, then made, then retracted. At first, we joked about it. We accepted the difficulty.

But the relationship deteriorated—eventually, the client owed us six figures. Not only was this money several months late, the company was unwilling to put forth any plan for paying us what we were owed.

No apology, no good faith, no repayment strategy, no *nothing*. And yet, the client expected us to keep working.

As a relatively good-natured and non-confrontational person, I did not know how to deal with this situation. There was a lot on the line, because this was a high-revenue job for our studio, and we had already *done* so much of the work, so it wasn't easy just to walk away. We were angry but we wanted our money, so we kept working and let our frustration simmer under the surface.

When I spoke to the CEO of the client company on the phone, he'd simply say, "We cannot pay, and quite frankly I'm disappointed that you are being so demanding."

Payment never came. Explanations never came. Even getting so much as an excuse out of them was like pulling teeth.

As the project went on I had many more uncomfortable conversations with the company's executives. The tension on our conference calls was so awkward it was almost funny. Almost. I strategized different ways to tactfully say, "Until you get caught up on payment, we'll need to discontinue the work." It never came out right. I lost sleep. I called our lawyer.

With a couple of swift and mysterious actions, our lawyer made the payment appear. Hocus pocus.

Then we fired the client.

After all that psychological and financial stress, I audited myself. What message had we sent to this client that made them think it was OK to walk all over us? What could we have done to prevent such a stressful eight months, and more importantly, *how could we become a studio with a well-earned reputation for delivering amazing work and receiving timely payment?*

Turns out, we could do a lot.

It became clear to me that this wasn't a unique situation with a demon client—this was a common occurrence (although handled uncommonly poorly by me) that most every creative professional has been through.

I wanted to fix it. For everyone. Why not? I had already lived through the worst case scenario, and had learned something valuable.

This feeling took me back to my days as a pro BMX rider,[2] when I'd be up against a 20-stair handrail, cameras running. Scared and trembling, after a few false starts, I'd give it a first try. Miss the rail, straddle it instead. Straight to my crotch at high speed. Then my shoulder would hit the fifth stair and I'd somersault down the remaining fifteen.

Any BMXer or skateboarder or other such "action sports athlete" will tell you that the feeling of lying in a crumpled heap at the bottom of 20 stairs is not the worst feeling in the world. The worst feeling in the world is not having tried. Trying and failing miserably is actually a relief. "OK. That was the thing I was afraid of. Now it's done. Next try has to be better, because it can't get worse." After the first fail, you are more determined. Almost encouraged. It can't get worse than the first try.

So after my monumental failure with the French client, I decided that I was going to get really, really good at this thing, that I would learn these "business management" skills that seem to be the bane of every creative professional's existence.

Plus, I had just watched six seasons of Ray Donovan and was very much romanticizing a potential new life as a fixer.

I read books about negotiation and communication. I drilled my lawyer with questions. I asked other successful studios and freelancers about their experiences. I learned correct procedures and put them into

---

2. https://www.youtube.com/watch?v=7z-pgjPRLAQ

practice. I overcame my fear of direct conversations. I got comfortable being uncomfortable. I began creating bulletproof proposals, scopes, and contracts. And most importantly, I developed trusting relationships, eliminating 90% of the miscommunication and awkwardness I had previously thought inevitable.

I studied how to appeal to the good and navigate the bad in each client, so that we could mitigate the bad stuff and spend more of our time on the good stuff.

We restored peace in the studio, and my creative partners returned to being creative. Our rates went up. We began earning a reputation among our peers for getting paid in full and on time.

I was so energized by this turnaround that I began helping other design studios and freelancers who were encountering the same problems I had struggled with. It went well beyond getting paid on schedule—these problems were about creatives not understanding the game, or the value of their work, or the amount of leverage they had. What do you do when your day rate is $500 but should be $1,200? What do you do when you really want the job but are afraid that your price quote will scare away the client? When the client pummels you with requests for extra work that was not agreed upon? When the client wants an endless number of revisions? Or asks you to start work before the contract is signed? Or asks you to cut your quote in half to meet their budget? And then misses the payment deadline anyway?

How can someone prevent all of these problems from occurring in the first place, and how does anyone make a proper living as a freelancer?

My messy experience taught me that the answer boils down to behavior. Talent is great, intelligence is helpful, but behavior is king. No matter what kind of freelancing work you do—design, photography, editing, writing—there are universal principles for creatives trying to make money from their art, and I will detail them for you in this book.

Diving into helping others, I learned that many, many creative people are underpaid, paid late, or otherwise taken advantage of. Sometimes clients really are out to get more for less, but more often, clients want to do what's right but aren't given good guidance from the freelancer. Creative freelancers who have the right mindset and learn to control the process will see that these events are not so inevitable as they seem.

This is not going to be about fighting against The Man, or demanding your worth because you're mad as hell and you're not going to take it anymore. It's about calmly taking control. Learning the rules so you can break them. Understanding the game so you can adjust your approach and let success happen.

4 Release Your Guilt

"You have a right to your labor, but not to the fruits of your labor."

— Krishna

Making art and commanding high prices for your art are two different things. This book assumes that you've already confirmed your identity as an artist. In doing so, you've surrendered to Krishna's statement.

You make art, period. New sentence. You receive money. That's an art in itself, which we will explore here.

In this book when we refer to art, we are talking about anything that you produce because you feel a divine need to produce it. Building software, writing words, painting colors, taking photos, art direction, fashion designing, landscaping, manscaping, roasting coffee (or "turning hot water brown" as coffee guru Tyler Wells[3] reverently refers to his craft). Whatever.

We are all creative. It's part of our identity as humans. Some suppress their creativity in exchange for a steady paycheck doing a mechanical job. Some produce creativity in a confined scope as someone else's employee. Some squeeze their creativity in on weekends.

Still others, and this includes you, create simply because they must.

You were born to do it. It comes through you, not from you. This, not money, is the reason you do what you do. Money is a byproduct. As such, money must be commanded in a way that does not diminish your ability to create, but also does not foster resentment.

You must emotionally detach your money from your art. This way, you let art come through you and money come to you.

The biggest threat to your art is the conflict that rises from negatively associating it with money.

If you sell the things you create in exchange for sums of money, and those sums are not substantial and appropriate, your art could suffer. Resentment will build, whether from *inaction* (telling yourself that's just

---

3. https://www.instagram.com/freakinalltime/

how it is), or *improper action* (bulldozing clients with your resentment, or passive aggressively muttering about how nobody respects your worth).

Once you've decided that selling your art will be your exclusive income, you should make peace with the fact that art, although still art, is *your job*. Its value to others is not reduced because you enjoy making it, or because making it came naturally to you.

There is no shame in creating because you need to express yourself, and working because you need to pay bills. Those things could remain separate forever. But if you have chosen to combine these two things, this book is for you.

If you have any remaining guilt associated with accepting the maximum possible amount of money in exchange for your art, I recommend that you shed it right now.

From this point forward I'll assume that all of us intend to live indoors, eat good food, and stack money for the future.

■ ■

Now, for a moment, set aside your own opinion of your work. What do your clients and peers say about you?

Do you deliver on time? Do you deliver early? Do you provide a value in excess of the price you charge? Are you a pleasure to speak with?

If you're a photographer, what environment do you create on set?

If you're a designer, how organized is your calendar of deliverables?

If you're a creative director, how do you package your services?

Are you impeccable with your word?

If an independent party surveyed all of your previous clients about you, would you post the results on Instagram or Twitter or LinkedIn?

If you're good at the thing you do, you are 20% of the way to making proper money as a freelancer. By the end of this book, you'll be well on your way to answering these questions with confidence—and any guilt you associate with collecting money will soon be behind you.

5   The Benefits of Freelancing

> *"Freedom is the top of luxury. When I went back to couture [at*
> *Chanel], I went back with the idea of freedom. You cannot buy*
> *me, but you can rent me! I'm a hired gun but I know how to*
> *handle guns. It's the only thing I want!"*
>
> — Karl Lagerfeld

I once managed 28 people at a medium-sized company. They were mostly creatives. About a third of them were freelancers. Most of those freelancers (except for the highest performers, ironically) were constantly asking me when they could become full-time employees. Why? They wanted "benefits."

I broke it down for them. The "benefits" of becoming an official employee of the company?

1. Having a portion of your health insurance paid.
2. Permission to participate in a 401(k) program which, statistically,[4] less than half of millennials will do.

Other benefits include: relinquishing the freedom to do other work and make more money, reducing your income streams down to one (you know, for "security"), losing control of your own time, and maybe (in some companies) being thrust into the game of corporate politics where vying for a promotion can become more important than being effective at your job.

As a freelancer, you value your ability to set your own pricing and hours, diversify your income streams, make more money, create your own schedule, and save profits on top of what you pay yourself.

I informed my freelancers that to make them an employee would cost the company about 150% of their compensation.

In other words, if your salary is $80K, it costs me $120K to have you as an employee (because of payroll tax, assorted red tape, and semi-antiquated expenses such as large offices).

---

4. https://www.businessinsider.com/
   millennials-saving-for-retirement-nearly-surpasses-gen-x-2019-11

This means that you, assuming you are great at what you do and everyone knows it, can set your price 50% higher than the market standard salary, because paying you more is still cheaper than hiring a true employee in your place, and your boss has the added benefit of zero commitment (as do you).

And that's just the minimum. If you're better, faster, and more pleasant than the full-time employee equivalent, companies are likely to pay you even more, and gladly.

As a company man, was it a bit strange for me to be this honest with my employees and freelancers? Maybe. But it's a rough world and life takes money and earning money takes savvy. I believed that the company could benefit from having some savvy professionals working there. It did.

Fast forward to now, I spend my days placing exemplary talent[5] into leadership roles at top fashion, lifestyle, and CPG brands, both full-time and freelance. That is to say, I absolutely believe that working for a company or working to leverage your freelance work into full-time employment are legitimate, valid paths. I also believe that most of the attitudes and behavior advocated in this book can be helpful for non-freelancers. The employee of the future is an entrepreneur within a company framework—someone who is flexible, understands what they're bringing to the table, and values personal relationships. Someone who can work independently, manage up,[6] and provide a value that is exponentially higher than the cost of employing them. Some of the best creative leaders have a background in freelance.

In other words, what you learn here will prepare you for most anything and allow you to keep your options open.

---

5. https://www.introlimited.com

6. https://www.tinypulse.com/blog/what-does-it-mean-to-manage-up

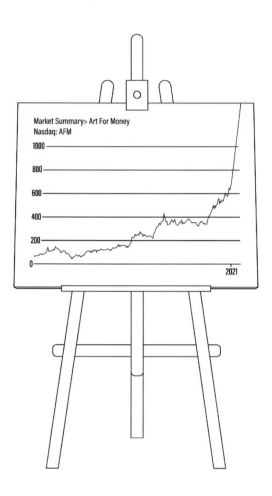

6 Price Your Work

> "*Self-respect is a discipline, a habit of mind that can never be faked but can be developed, trained.*"
>
> — Joan Didion

6.1 *Value Yourself*

With all of that said, as a freelancer, putting a price on your work can be difficult. Every freelancer has an anecdote about a friend of a friend who bills premium rates, and gets paid every time. Why does she get her asking price, and you don't? Be careful not to brush off that person's success as luck or good marketing. In part, it may be those things, and that's OK. But there's probably a story there. What is she doing differently? What is the client seeing when they look at her?

Most likely the client sees results, delivered on time, by someone who articulates and carries herself well, backed by a good reputation.

And there's probably even more to the story than that. In my experience, the cheapest clients are also the highest-maintenance clients. When they see how willing you are to bend over backward for their endless requests for out-of-scope favors, they will pile them on. Why wouldn't they? It's their job to get the most for the least. On the flip side, great clients with healthy budgets tend to understand quality and pay accordingly without too much fuss.

Successful freelancers not only know this, but back it up with action. This is risky. You have to know your value and believe in it enough to quote a respectable price, and be ready to walk away if the client can't afford you. *How* you walk away is important. Be friendly and cool and express interest in staying in touch.

You have to know that those clients who can't afford you will at least respect your professionalism and your price, and they'll remember how pleasant and excited you were. They'll come back to you in the future when they have money, or they'll recommend you to someone who already does. This happens often.

Clients regularly encounter freelancers who are out of their price range. There are freelancers out there doing great work and getting paid great money for it. Like them, you want to stand out from everyone else by offering a unique overall package that no one else can replicate—not by simply being cheaper.

6.2 *Determining Target Revenue*

> *"When you argue for your limitations, you get to keep them."*
>
> — Jim Kwik

If you want to make proper money as a freelancer, it's important to not avert your gaze and say "Uuuuhhhhhh" when someone asks you how much you charge.

Professionals know how to field this question: with a calm smile, they say, "Sure, tell me more about what you need and I'll get you a quote by noon tomorrow."

To do this, professional creatives need a fast, bulletproof method for calculating a quote. There are two ways to create that method:

If you're an experienced freelancer, take the total amount of money you made last year (or whatever was your best year to date) and divide it by 2,080 (the number of business hours in a year). *This is now the minimum value of one hour of your time.* This can serve not only as your starting point for pricing out jobs, but also—and I'm going to get a little philosophical here—it's *your measuring stick for how you should be spending your time in general.*

Let's say, hypothetically, that you made $88 per hour last year. You want to improve this year, so now your baseline is $100 per hour.

Think about what that means. It means that from now on, whenever you spend an hour on something that could have been outsourced for less than $100 (or not done at all), you are throwing away money. Instead of throwing away money, I humbly recommend that you channel that time into your art. When you show yourself that level of respect, it's easier to expect your clients to do the same.

Now let's get back to pricing.

If you don't already know your **target revenue** for the year, no problem. Let's create it right now.

Years ago, one of my mentors (previously a CEO and now a successful investor) broke down for me the basics of how to price freelance services. I listened carefully and took notes furiously, because A) he's an intimidatingly smart man who would shout when teaching me business fundamentals, and B) he had used these fundamentals to earn himself some of the same things I wanted out of life (control of his own time and a vintage Ferrari collection, to name a few).

So, I put those basics into an Excel model which spits out a quote based on the answers to a few simple questions:

1. What would your annual income be if you were employed, at your current level of experience, by a healthy sized company? (If you're unsure, I'd skip most of the online articles about this, and instead make friends with a recruiter and ask them). Add 50% to that number, for reasons outlined in The Benefits of Freelancing.§5
2. What are your fixed and variable monthly expenses related to your freelance work?
3. Do you have anyone working for you and what do you pay them?

Toss the above numbers, along with an estimate of hours you plan to spend on a given project, into this Excel model[7] and out comes a cost.

---

7. https://www.holloway.com/afm-model

Here's what that looks like, using made-up numbers for illustrative purposes:

- You're a copywriter who made $75K in your last full-time role.
- $75K plus 50% is $112,500 per year. Your deductible rent is $6K per year (you can consult an accountant to to find this number, or estimate[8] how much you can deduct), you spend roughly $7K on hourly assistant help, and you have $8K in additional business expenses, so your annual overhead is $21K.
- Your new total target revenue is $133,500.
- There are 2080 business hours in the year. Your base hourly rate is $133,500 divided by 2080, or roughly $64 per hour.

Now you know that it costs *at least* $64 for you to do work for an hour.

◇ IMPORTANT *This is not your quote.* It's your starting point. It's the minimum amount of money you'd need to charge in order to pay yourself, your people, and your expenses. If you take less than this price, you are either discounting your hourly value, or worse, losing money. Think carefully about what a client thinks of a freelancer who jumps at the chance to lose money. Think carefully about yourself, your training, and the quality of your work. Remember that you may not actually be collecting money for every single one of those 2080 hours you have available to work.

6.3 *Determining Retail Value*

The next thing to determine is the **retail value** of the work you are going to deliver. You can do this by Googling, knowing your industry, talking regularly with your peers, reflecting on your past experience, understanding your client's financial goals, and consulting with mentors.

Graphic designers have the Pricing and Ethical Guidelines[9] to reference; your industry might offer something similar. As you gather data on other peoples' rates and salaries, keep in mind that some people may not be paid fairly, so some data may be more noise than signal.

---

8. https://bench.co/blog/tax-tips/home-office-deduction/
9. https://graphicartistsguild.org/product/
   the-graphic-artists-guild-handbook-pricing-ethical-guidelines/

Part of the beauty of freelance work is that you get to decide what's fair. On the flip side, the market will keep you honest. If a client is asking you to create a logo, for example, chances are they've asked others to quote the same job, and their reaction to your quote will give you an indication of whether it's over or under the market. This is just another data point of course, not an absolute truth, but after a few failed attempts at charging $10K for a branding job, you might learn that charging $7K is actually more lucrative for you, because at this price you'll actually be working.

6.4 *Creating Your Quote*

Your quote needs to be somewhere between your **cost basis** and the **retail value** of the work. That difference is your **profit margin**, which is the money that stays in your business savings account until you either need it for an emergency or it's time to pay yourself a bonus, whichever comes first.

Play with margins, shooting for 50%, in your Excel model until you settle on a quote that matches the retail value of the work. Make it precise, and not too round in number.

When you put out your first quote, it is not unlikely that the client will come back to you with a startled tone and a story about budget constraints. Don't be mad. This is part of the dance, and now it's your turn.

You will respond with a smile and an, "OK, well let's revisit the scope[§7.5] and see what we can adjust." Your tone is unfazed and cool, because you know that there are only two outcomes, and both are good.

- **Outcome #1:** You remove some items from the scope and allow yourself to (scientifically, not arbitrarily) reduce your price, because now you're doing less work for less money, and the client agrees.
- **Outcome #2:** The client can't (or won't) pay even your reduced price, at which point you get to evaluate if they're worth working with.

6.5 *Should You Just Bill Hourly?*

You may ask, *why don't I just keep it simple and bill all my clients on an hourly basis?* It seems fair and easy. It's not wrong to do that—you can incrementally raise the value of your time as you grow and improve.

However, in practice, most freelancers are not well served by billing at a simple hourly rate.

First, you are an artist, and it is highly unlikely that every single hour of your work requires the same skill and effort—or delivers the same value. For example, you might be helping a client with a new strategy for a product that could transform the company, while also doing some copy editing for the website. Billing a fixed hourly rate makes it difficult to vary your pricing based on the importance (retail value to the customer) of the work.

Second, you can't price jobs in a way that accounts for all of your own internal costs, which are not static day to day.

Finally, it matters how much the client is committing to: the overall size of the job. There is way more overhead to working ten 4-hour jobs for ten clients than one 40-hour job for one client. You're doing ten times the sales efforts, on top of the mental gymnastics. A short engagement *costs you* more per hour than a long one. If the scope is starting small but might expand, you can quote a higher rate but explain that you'd be glad to consider a lower rate once the larger commitment is clear.

When you price a job, the first step of your calculation should be to cover your own hours, but your ultimate goal should be to deliver an incredible result at a price that reflects the value you deliver—that's what your client really cares about.

Trading your time for money isn't the worst thing in the world when you're starting out, but you want to work toward decoupling your "input" and "output." If the quality of your work is excellent and your approach is unique, you'll create scenarios where your output (the price a client must pay you because no one else can do what you do) is much higher than your input (the hours you spent creating). God bless your grandparents for working the same job for 50 years for flat hourly wages. But this shall not be your destiny.

There are exceptions to every rule; use your own judgement based on the nature of your art. A writer might be paid by the word, for example. But keep in mind the value your words are delivering, and on what scale. A post for your cousin's blog, although valuable, will impact the world differently than a piece for the *Times*.

In conclusion, your hours should be tracked and you should internally assign value to them, but keep a flexible relationship between your estimated hours and your client quote:

- Prices should reflect the true value to the client.
- Prices should reflect your overall expenses.
- Smaller jobs should cost more per hour, while larger commitments earn a lower rate.
- Prices can reflect your other priorities and convenience.

This will allow you to work on a variety of big and small projects while keeping your prices fair.

6.6 *Offering Discounts*

There are a few reasons why a freelancer like you would consider discounting your work for a client:

- **You need money.** You're desperate. But like the wise Sheriff in Super Troopers says, "Desperation is a stinky cologne." If you cave in easily when it comes to your value, you are only learning to agree to what you're offered, rather than learning what might be possible. And with the stink of desperation on you, you'll be offered even less. Keep cool and you could walk away with more than you're willing to accept.
- **You want this client longer term.** You believe this client could be a great long-term partner for you, and you want to start off by making them happy. However, what they're willing to pay you on your first job is highly indicative of what they're willing to pay you on every job, ever.
- **You want to build a portfolio.** You're just starting out, and you want to take on as much work as possible to build up your portfolio and get referrals. If this is the case, it's a legitimate choice. But make sure you revisit the above calculations each year and give yourself a regular raise.
- **You care about the client.** You really like the client, you believe in their brand, or they're personal friends or family. In any of these cases, still quote them full price. If your full price quote is out of their budget, they'll come back to you and say so. Or, if you know for a fact that your price is out of their budget, you can preemptively write a friends

and family discount into the invoice, *making sure they see the full price quote next to it*, in order to set a fact-based high bar regarding your value. Negotiators call this "anchoring."

On the flip side of the latter situation, sometimes you'll be asked to do jobs that you simply don't want to do, or for a client that you might not feel a strong sense of closeness or obligation to. In these cases, you can easily use your **pricing model** to dial up the margin for the job. Not enough to gouge them, but enough to make you more enthused about doing the job, and creating a financial cushion that could enable you to dial down the margin for deserving clients on the other end of the spectrum. Do this ethically and you can actually create win-win pricing scenarios: if they say yes, you make a lot of money, and if they say no, you don't have to do the job.

Consider the above reasons carefully, and if you reach a point where it's pretty clear that the client does not intend to pay you anywhere near your rate, I encourage you to smile and say, "Well, thanks anyway for thinking of me, and let's stay in touch. I love your brand and I hope we can find a way to work together in the future."

Does this sound like leaving dollars on the table? It is, and for good reason.

Consider the alternative: you cave to the client's budget, you deliver, and what do you think happens next? The client comes to you with the next job and brings more money this time?

Nope. The client has identified you as the bargain option in the marketplace, and you can bet that every time they need big work for small money, they'll come right back to you.

You can also bet that within the company, when your name comes up, it will be accompanied by words like "inexpensive" and "works with us on budget" and maybe even "cheap." These are not words you want associated with your art.

⬦ **CAUTION** Think carefully about what a client thinks about a freelancer whose default mode is to immediately offer a discount. Make them ask for it.

Even if you aren't necessarily in love with the client or their brand and you just simply need the money, you have an ace up your sleeve–you can actually go down in price without losing money.

Once you know that the client needs a discount from you, there's nothing wrong with offering it. The important thing is properly communicating the discount. And that doesn't mean fabricating some pretend pricing just to show that you're giving them a discount. Use your pricing model, and make it real.

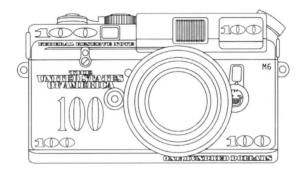

7 Writing a Good Proposal

*"We are kept from our goal not by obstacles but by a clear path to
a lesser goal."*

— Robert Brault

7.1 *A Sample Proposal*

Freelancers find themselves in lots of difficult situations. A client isn't giving you enough time, your payment is arriving late, you don't have any leverage to get your money, you're being coerced into providing more services than you signed up for.

The vast majority of these situations can be prevented by creating an impeccable proposal.

A properly written proposal should be about two pages long. Enough detail to provide clarity and protect you from misunderstanding, but not so long that it's intimidating. Done well, your proposal can eliminate the majority of nightmare outcomes. Your client will hesitate before asking for extra revisions in the middle of the engagement not just because your proposal outlined how many revisions are included in the price, but also because the proposal will professionally convey the fact that your time and services are in demand and valuable. This is good for them to know. They want to know it. It gives them comfort.

Easy on the Extras, Inc.
1234 Main Street
Los Angeles, CA 12345

EASY ON THE EXTRAS

CLIENT:
FICTIONAL NAME, INC
ATTN: Trip Fontaine
1234 Maple Street
New York, NY 12345

PROJECT PROPOSAL:
FOOTWEAR DESIGN 1
January 1st, 2021

CLIENT CONTACT:
Trip Fontaine

SCOPE IN:
The below services are included in this agreement and fee estimate

CONCEPT - 2 weeks
Create direction brief based on client mood board
Meeting #1: client reviews and provides feedback

SKETCHING - 6 weeks
Perform a maxiumum of two rounds of Concept revisions
Create basic drawings to convey design intent
Meeting #2: client reviews and provides feedback

TECH PACKS - 4 weeks
Perform a maximum of two rounds of revisions
Create tech packs based on client's approval of sketches
Include all necessary information for factory
Meeting #3: client reviews tech packs and provides final feedback

SCOPE OUT:
Per client advice 1/1/2021, the below services are not requested or included

IDEATION
Client has already completed concept

DEVELOPMENT
Client prefers to manage development, sampling, vendor comments and approvals

FACTORY COMMUNICATION
Client prefers to perform factory visits, costing and all other
communication to finalize production sample

EASY ON THE EXTRAS

Easy on the Extras, Inc.
1234 Main Street
Los Angeles, CA 12345

CLIENT:
FICTIONAL NAME, INC
ATTN: Trip Fontaine
1234 Maple Street
New York, NY 12345

PROJECT PROPOSAL:
FOOTWEAR DESIGN I
January 1st, 2021

CLIENT CONTACT:

Trip Fontaine

PAYMENT SCHEDULE

Project total: $31,500

15% Friends/Family reduction: $26,775

Rush fee: N/A

Deposit due upon start of work: $8,925

Due at or before meeting #2: $8,925

Balance due upon delivery of final assets: $8,925

SIGNED

If this proposal is executed, it will serve as the partnership agreement, which begins on the date of deposit receipt and ends after 12 weeks, or upon completion of deliverables in scope, whichever comes first.

Both parties agree that the project timeline is based on receipt of timely approvals by client (within five days of submission).

If approval time extends beyond five days, design timeline will also require an extension which is subject to hourly or daily rates. Additional services not outlined in this agreement, or added after start of work, are subject to a change-order which may require additional timeline and budget.

Any expenses incurred by designer on client's behalf will be submitted to client for reimbursement. Expenses over $250 will require prior approval by client.

CLIENT   DESIGNER

NAME: NAME:
COMPANY NAME: COMPANY NAME:
SIGNATURE: SIGNATURE:
TITLE: TITLE:
PHONE NUMBER: PHONE NUMBER:
EMAIL: EMAIL:
DATE: DATE:

A good proposal sends two messages:

- The first message is straight-forward. "Here is my understanding of the work you have asked me to do for you, and how much it will cost." That part is expected.
- The second message is more subliminal, and comes across in the beauty, language, and specificity of the proposal. That message is, "I have great value and I know how to deliver it on a specific timeline in exchange for precise amounts of money. You will be very happy that you hired me. Indeed, I have done this many times before."

Depending on how long you've been freelancing, you may already have a proposal format you use. It probably contains:

- Your logo and business name at the top.
- A summary of the services you plan to provide.
- A total dollar amount you wish to receive in return.

If you're a little more advanced, you might do these as well:

- Name the project, if the client hasn't already. No need to get creative here. Client name plus two words describing what you're doing for them. Under the name, in one or two sentences, summarize the needs of the client and what you plan to deliver.
- List the deliverables. This is everything the client expects you to hand off to them, and everything you need from the client in order to do so.

You can get away with just having the first three, or include all five to show you're a serious player. But if you want to avoid all of the painful situations listed above, if you really want to wow your clients and build long-term relationships with them, and if you want to stand out in your field as the most professional freelancer imaginable, one who can command high rates because they make everything easier for their clients and leave nothing to doubt, you must add these to your proposal:

- Touch points—when will you check in with your client?
- Phases of work
- Pricing structure
- Scope of work
- Fee structure

Let's go through those now.

7.2 *Touch Points*

As part of your proposal, list the touch points—that is, the moments over the course of the project where you (and/or your team) will engage in a planned conversation with the client (and/or their team). The purpose of these touch points might be to hand off the deliverables, ask questions, or give a general update on the progress. Over-communication is key, because, as James Altucher[10] says, "Most people are 8-year olds."

This is not an insult to anyone, it's the reality of dealing with busy, stressed, insecure, distracted human beings, some of whom don't care a lot about their jobs. You might be dealing with one person, or more likely, a team of people who don't talk to each other. They are never listening as closely as you think they are, so you need to repeat yourself.

This might sound annoying. Get over that, and quickly. Just master it. It's not hard, and it will reward you exponentially. Get in touch with the client over the course of the project, rather than waiting for them to get in touch with you. Even if there's nothing to report, just say a quick "hi" and remind them what you're bringing to the next touchpoint.

7.3 *Phases of Work*

Break down the phases of work. Even the simplest job can be broken into smaller pieces that are easy for your client to understand and easy for you to deliver.

The objective of breaking the job into phases is to give your client a quick inside look at what goes into this stuff. Let's say a client asks you to create a logo for her business. For simplicity's sake, let's say this client's business is small, and she's a bit less experienced when it comes to working with creatives. We'll call her Tanya.

When Tanya first contacted you, she had a certain idea in her head. You asked her what she was interested in seeing, and she says that she wants something clean and modern but also retro and classic and also a little edgy. When you ask her to show you references (existing logos that she's attracted to) she says, "It's in my head. I'll know it when I see it."

Then Tanya imagines that you'll take two hours to churn out 30 various logo options for her to critique, and then you'll have an ongoing conversation for an undefined number of days while you produce limitless revisions until she sees something she likes, and then she'll pay you, maybe.

By the end, some quick math will tell you, retrospectively, that your hourly rate for Tanya's project was six dollars.

---

10. https://jamesaltucher.com

The phases of work section of your proposal is your chance to avoid that nightmare by taking a valuable opportunity to educate the client. Chop it up something like this:

- **Phase One: Concept**

  - *3 days*
  - Client provides references.
  - Artist presents Mood Board and Graphic Concepts.
  - Client agrees on direction within 5 days from start.

- **Phase Two: Creation**

  - *5 days*
  - Artist presents three possible Graphic Directions.
  - Client chooses one direction.
  - Based on agreed direction, Artist builds out three explorations: Logo, Wordmark, Lockup.

- **Phase Three: Finalization**

  - *3 days*
  - Client chooses their preferred logo, wordmark, and lockup from the directions presented in Phase 2.
  - Up to 3 revisions are made as Artist refines each.
  - Balance payment is due.
  - Assets are handed off in the preferred format.

This should take up one page of the proposal. For a more complex project, this could take multiple pages, but the bulleted style and concise language keeps it clear and manageable. Don't overwhelm Tanya with complexity, just include what she needs to know.

Laying out the phases like this achieves a few things: First, your client now has a picture of all the steps involved in creating her logo. "Wow, this takes lots of skilled work, and I play a part in the process!" she says to herself as she realizes that her participation is expected at key moments throughout.

You'll notice that this appears to be an 11-day project in total, but that no dates are mentioned, and each phase's timeline is dependent upon the timely execution of the previous phase. And that timely execution depends in part on your client.

This project could take 11 days or 33 days—that's up to Tanya. The workload for you is the same either way. It's probably in your (and Tanya's) best interest to do the project in as few days as possible, so you have the opportunity up front to encourage her to think through her references and provide them to you with urgency, because the clock on her project doesn't start until she does.

The above is for a pretty straight-forward project, but you can imagine how the steps and details I'm outlining here are even more crucial when you're dealing with a bigger project, or a larger team of Tanyas.

After the final phase, summarize the total project timeline, again avoiding dates—start and end dates can be added when the agreement is signed. Until then, speak in days or weeks.

Most importantly, at the bottom of the total project timeline, add this: *"Work begins when client has sent all references for the work, agreement is executed, and deposit is received."* Perhaps your work doesn't require references, but include anything you need from the client here, and name it.

7.4 *Pricing Structure*

Generally speaking (and this will vary according to the specific services you offer) it's best not to present an a la carte menu of options with price tags on each service. If you do, the client will pick and choose in the way that leaves you with the least possible amount of money, and holes in the final outcome. For example, imagine you're a pattern maker. A client wants to pay you to create and submit patterns, but not approve fit samples. Now you've got a final product entering the world, potentially with your name on it, that someone else has likely screwed up.

If you can work on a project basis, do that, and, divide the project into phases, with a cost for each phase:

- 50% for phase 1
- 30% for phase 2
- 20% for phase 3

This front-loaded pricing model encourages the client to stick with the project because they've already paid you most of the money. Play with these percentages if you like, but I encourage you to ensure that the smallest payment is correlated with the final phase. The final phase is where clients are most likely to get off track, and if they've already invested substantially in the project, they'll be incentivized to continue being a great partner and finish clean. It also enables you to build a cash cushion and protect your business from risk, without having to demand an arbitrary up-front deposit or "start work fee," which can be difficult to explain to a client.

If you're applying a discount,$^{\S6.6}$ do so as a percentage and highlight it in your proposal. Before sending, call the client and let them know why you are extending this one-time friends and family discount (if you're doing the project at a discount because you love the brand or want the opportunity, you can still call it a "friends and family" discount—you want to be friends, right?). You have a personal interest in this project and you are willing to invest in this relationship.

The above may seem like a lot, but once the process becomes habit, you will be able to cruise through it pleasantly, quickly, and smoothly without exhausting yourself or your client.

With this in place, the "due date" of each payment will not be left up to the client's imagination. And, if for any reason the client fails to remit a payment, you hold the power: assets are exchanged at time of payment.

◇ **IMPORTANT** Important to note: tying a specific payment to a specific phase of work is not applicable to every type of freelancer. You might be a baker. Your client might think of it like the Mitch Hedburg joke: "I give you the money, you give me the donut! End of transaction."[11] And this is rightfully so. The easier you make it for your client to pay you, the more likely you are to get paid.

The main principle here is that when you are investing up-front time and effort into a client project, it is prudent to require that your client invest up-front as well. Use your judgement to create the system that's best for you. If you are dealing with a client who has proven troublesome in the past, you'll want to do your best to tie payment to deliverables, so you can deliver the work after payment has cleared your account.

This all may seem harsh, and yes, if you wait until there's a problem before sharing these guidelines, they *are* harsh.

---

11. https://www.youtube.com/watch?v=gWx6uA5aCrE

But if they're part of the proposal, and you review the proposal verbally in a nice "to keep everything clear and easy I'll just walk you through the process" tone of voice before kicking off the project, your client will appreciate it, and respect you.

7.5 *Scope Your Work*

Often omitted from a proposal, to the detriment of everyone involved, is the **scope of work**, or **SOW**.

Sometimes the SOW is present, but lacking. Your SOW should be broken into two sections:

- **Scope In** is the list of services that the client is asking for.
- **Scope Out** is the list of services that you are capable of, but the client is not currently asking for.

As you likely already know, there's a 75% chance that the client *does not know* what services they need at the time of hiring you, and to save money, are erring on the side of "as few as possible." This is OK with you, because you're equipped to deal with the panic that will arise a few weeks into the project, when the client realizes they need more of your services. You say: "No problem! Let's revisit the SOW, and we'll work this out."

You can now sit with the client and move the additional services from "Scope Out" to "Scope In," and kindly explain the cost of each service. That cost, of course, is now a bit higher than it would have been if the client had asked for them as part of the original package. (It's best to explain this at the beginning, not right now.) The reason for this is that you are now in a rush.

As Seth Godin says,[12] "panic costs extra," so you need a standard "rush fee" ready to apply whenever a client adds work without adding time. It's not because we're mad that the client added work—we love work! But losing sleep in order to deliver your best work should be an exception, not a norm.

The purpose of "Scope In" and "Scope Out" is to give your client the chance to order all the services they need up front, rather than waiting until the end to pile on. You're doing this to help yourself (to avoid panic,

---

12. https://seths.blog/2018/08/emergencies-cost-extra/

or at least be compensated for it) and to help the client (giving them a fair chance to reduce their cost and their stress).

In many cases, it's difficult for the client to foresee every single service that they will need, and flexibility on your part is always expected and appropriate. Being clear about this upfront will plant an understanding in the client's memory that, although they are perfectly welcome to do this, it will cost money, and that's OK because it's agreed and understood beforehand.

If the client requesting a late-add of services is a friend or a VIP who, for whatever reason, you feel should get those additional services for free, no problem! Still, you will ceremoniously move the additional services from "Scope Out" to "Scope In," list the price for each service, cross out the price, and itemize each service at $0 as "complimentary."

It's important for your client to know that these services are valuable. It won't be OK for them to pay you a flat fee and then milk you limitlessly for the term of your contract. They know this deep down, but they need your SOW to *show* them. They will appreciate the education and they will appreciate being in the hands of a professional.

7.6 *Final Fees*

The very end of the proposal is a short list of the fees we haven't addressed yet.

7.6.1 DAY RATE AND HOURLY RATE

The likelihood of a client causing this project to go overtime is high, and you do not want to eat that cost. That's why you have a **day rate** in your back pocket—the amount of money you require for a full day of dedicated overtime work. (If the work takes the majority of a day, you'll charge your day rate. If it takes less, you might bill a half day.)

It should read something like: *"Any services not outlined in this proposal or required after [end date here] may be commissioned from [your name here] at the rate of [day rate here] per day."*

To calculate your day rate, just divide the project fee by the number of days in the project, then add a small percentage, something like 20%. You don't want your day rate to be so low that it incentivizes your client to avoid committing to full projects.

Unless you work solely on a day rate basis, your day rate is for special situations only.

Your **hourly rate**[§6.5] is the same, but take your day rate, divide it by 8, then add 20%. You don't want your hourly to be so low that it incentivizes your client to avoid committing to full days.

7.6.2 TRAVEL FEES

A day of travel should be billed at your regular day rate, plus expenses. Keep in mind that clients, when they send you on an all-expense paid trip to do a project for them, expect that you'll be fully dedicated to their project while you're there on their dime. As such, make sure that the day rate you quote is high enough to accommodate the fact that you likely won't be able to squeeze in any other client work after-hours. If you're the type of freelancer who's constantly working on multiple projects at once, then paid travel days could potentially *cost* you money, so consider making your "travel day rate" a bit higher than your regular day rate.

7.6.3 EXPENSES

To spare you a long list, I'll just state that *any expenditure that the client requires you to make on their behalf* (reference samples are a common example in the design world; fill in your own as needed) should be submitted to the client in an expense report, separately from your invoice, so that the money comes back to you as reimbursement, and not as taxable pay. Pick a reasonable dollar amount ($250) and state in the proposal that any expenses over that amount will need pre-approval from the client. The client may have their own dollar amount already established for such situations as this. Go with it.

7.7 *Client Contact*

One last thing that often gets overlooked: name your client contact at the bottom of the proposal. This is the person to whom you report. You don't take direction from anyone other than this person (like the late fees thing, be reasonably flexible in the spirit of partnership), especially if it's conflicting direction. Tanya doesn't get to take off on a 2-week vacation, leaving Brendan in charge, then return from vacation and override everything

Brendan said so you can do two extra weeks of free work because of their miscommunication.

7.8 *Create Your Contract*

> *"Design trumps willpower."*
>
> — B.J. Fogg, Stanford psychologist

For smaller, lower-risk jobs, include a section at the end of your proposal that says, "If this proposal is executed, it becomes the agreement," with a dotted line for both parties to sign. Keep in mind that it may not hold up in court, so this solution is for smaller jobs with known clients, and it is only a viable option if your proposal is impeccable, with a very clear scope of work.§7.5

Whichever option you choose, don't start working until the agreement is signed.

⬦ CAUTION If this is a bigger job (meaning that failing to collect the full fee would jeopardize your business), then you need a full contract, and you need legal counsel.

I, your humble author, am not a lawyer, and thus this chapter does not constitute legal advice. My lawyer's name is, incredibly, Art. He speaks in facts, and he drives a Porsche 911. His hourly rate is not low, but there are good reasons I'm OK with that:

He's good at what he does and I learn from him. For every dollar I give him, I get knowledge that saves me two future dollars. He doesn't waste time. He makes just enough small talk so that you know he's a real person, and the rest is business. He's the one who got our money from the nightmare client from the start of the book, and he continues to save the day as needed.

You can pay a lawyer to draft you a contract from scratch, or you can be resourceful and find a great template, personalize it as best you can based on the type of services you provide, and then pay a lawyer to refine as needed.

Stress to your lawyer the importance of making the contract as succinct as possible (long contracts intimidate clients and delay forward progress) without leaving you vulnerable. I failed to do this once with a previous lawyer, and as a result ended up with a ridiculously verbose contract. I had to pay Art a thousand bucks to make it two pages shorter. It was worth it—clients sign quickly now.

The contract overview looks like:

- **A few pages** of normal contract content, setting up the basic rules of engagement, trade secrets, intellectual property, term, and termination. This section normally ends with "responsible parties" (you, and the person you're reporting to) and signatures. The remaining aspects of the contract are addenda.
- **Exhibit A, the work order.** This outlines the services and scope, and in some cases can be copied, or summarized, from your proposal and SOW.[§7.5] If you require special things from your client in order to do this job properly, list those things here.
- **Exhibit B, the payment schedule.** This is a more detailed version of the payment schedule[§7.4] you outlined in the proposal. It also includes the agreed rules about travel fees and expenses. These travel expenses, along with any other expenses you expect to incur (such as shipping, purchasing materials, reference samples, etc.) don't need to be pre-calculated, but their existence should be acknowledged up front and they must be reimbursed within a short period, such as 15 days. You are a creative professional, not a bank for your client to borrow from.
- Lastly, **late fees.** I recommend applying a 2.5% to 5% fee to late payments, and this late fee should compound monthly. (Recognize the difference between having a late fee policy and actually exercising it. Be careful and use friendly, human judgement. It's there to signal professionalism and protect you from flagrant abuse—not to sour a partnership with an otherwise great client who accidentally paid four days late.)

If you can, send the contract electronically, giving the client the fewest possible reasons not to sign quickly ("I don't have a printer handy" is a common one) so you can get started.

7.9 *Proposal Checklist*

- Quote the Job
  - Start with covering your own costs.

- Add a margin based on the industry standard retail value of the work.

- Write the Proposal

  - Include:

    - Scope
    - Phases
    - Key dates
    - Touch points
    - Fee quote
    - Name of contact

  - Create an agreement with your client around timing of payment.

- Create a Contract

  - Remember: For small jobs, a signed proposal is good. For big jobs, you need a full contract; have your template ready so it's quick and easy.

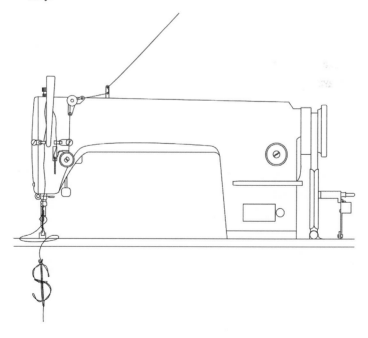

8 Doing The Job

"That which hinders your task, is your task."

— Sanford Meisner

8.1 *Clean Up Your Space*

Your workspace should be a peaceful place. How that looks is something you can define on your own, based on what makes you feel calm, what type of art you create, and what your needs are. Your workspace doesn't need to look like mine, but don't fool yourself into thinking a chaotic environment is working well for you. I've never met anyone who functioned well in a messy workspace. On the contrary, most people are anxious and have trouble focusing. *Do not miss the connection between mental and spatial chaos.* As Steven Pressfield wrote in *The War of Art*, "The Professional eliminates chaos from his world in order to banish it from his mind."

Whether you have an office, or a home office, or four square feet of your own in an apartment with six roommates, I urge you to optimize your little slice of real estate. Space is a luxury, however much of it you have. Being in it should feel great.

Order, for the creative professional's physical space, can be achieved in three steps:

- **Scale down.** The main reason that organizing is so daunting is that there's *so much* to organize. Easy fix: get rid of most of your shit. Throw it away, give it away, or sell it. Easy guidelines that have helped me: if you haven't used it in six months, get rid of it. If you're not sure whether you need it, get rid of it. If you haven't thought about it since the last time you saw it, get rid of it, and if it has sentimental value but isn't beautiful or useful, take a nice picture of it and then get rid of it. Amos Tversky said it best: "Unless you are kicking yourself once a month for throwing something away, you're not throwing enough away."

- **Organize what's left.** Consolidated clutter is less stressful than clutter sprinkled everywhere. Scanner Pro[13] allows you to scan papers from your phone straight into designated Dropbox folders. Evernote[14] makes it possible to save (and search and retrieve) every worthwhile thought you've ever had.

Paper is cool and all, but save it for special occasions. I once worked with someone who insisted on only taking notes on paper. Not a notebook—actual single pieces of paper. Now he has twelve years' worth of notes which are unsearchable and thus useless to him. On top of that, his office looks like a storage locker.[15] Guess how much work he gets done in a day?

What apps you choose don't matter; in most cases it's not worth spending an hour to research ways to save five minutes. The best system is one that you'll actually use. Pick your favorite or flip a coin.

- **Embrace it.** Now that you know where everything is, enjoy your new identity as an organized person. Working in a newly sorted space is like getting out of a UPS truck and into a Ferrari. You've traded your heavy baggage for horsepower. That feels good.

Is this whole "order" thing not working for you? Not what you grew up with? Not part of your personality? It's easy to assume that some people are just naturally tidy and organized. Not so. It happens on purpose.

If you are questioning how organized your space should be, just ask yourself, "How clear headed would I like to feel and how well do I want to perform?"

8.2 *Calendarize*

> "*Willpower is garbage. It is for amateurs. It's for people still conflicted about what they want to do.*"
>
> — Darren Hardy

---

13. https://readdle.com/scannerpro

14. https://evernote.com

15. https://www.chicagotribune.com/lifestyles/health/
sc-how-to-help-a-hoarder-health-0222-20170217-story.html

Every force of evil in the world is conspiring against you delivering this project on time. Whatever can go wrong, will go wrong. It will not be a thing that you expect. It will be a thing that is easy to blame on someone else. Don't fool yourself.

If you're the best photographer in Los Angeles and you deliver your projects three days late, what are you?

Not the best photographer in Los Angeles.

Your reputation is your ability to keep working. Your reputation is quickly destroyed when you deliver late. Your clients don't remember the beautiful lighting, the perfect retouching, or the fact that you made the models feel comfortable and brought out their best. What they'll remember—and what they'll tell their professional colleagues—is that you delivered late.

It's not hard to deliver on time. When you deliver late, it's almost never because you weren't talented enough or the work was too hard. It's usually because your "calendarization" was lacking.

Calendarizing, though not a real word, will make or break your project. It guides your workflow and it guides your client's expectations. It controls your anxiety and your client's anxiety. It gets you paid on time and makes everyone happy.

As illustrated in Writing a Good Proposal,$^{\S7.3}$ every project should be broken down into phases (which will appear in your proposal). Calendarize these phases by detailing what needs to be done to complete each phase, and marking them in your calendar for you and anyone else you are relying on for help on this project.

If a project is large or has a long lead time, we tend to relax at the beginning and thrash at the end. This is exactly the opposite of a good approach. To avoid tricking ourselves into thinking we have plenty of time to finish a project, focus on Phase 1. That's much shorter. And it has a real deadline. This encourages us to "Thrash Now, Ship Early,"[16] as Seth Godin preaches. Never thrash at the end. The end is stressful enough as it is.

Also, good news: you've already outlined the phases of work,$^{\S7.3}$ back when you made your proposal. So, all you're really doing now is applying dates to those phases.

---

16. https://podcasts.apple.com/nz/podcast/thrash-now/id1345042626?i=1000420016831

8.3 *Set Alerts and Deliver Early*

Whenever I've made an important commitment, I set two reminders: one on the day it's due, and another one three days in advance. Why do I do that? Isn't it simple to remember that X work needs to be done by X date? Yes it's simple, but simple ain't easy, and besides:

Never waste good brain space on something that your phone can easily do for you.

Alerts aren't just for deliverables; you can use them for payments as well. Remember, most people are 8-year-olds. We don't prepare for the things we don't enjoy doing. If we don't enjoy going to the dentist, then we are less likely to be on time.

Your client's accounts payable department doesn't enjoy paying you on time. As such, they most certainly do not have a pink sticky note on their monitor that reads "IMPORTANT NOTE TO SELF: pay Johnny Freelance on February 1st!" And that's perfectly fine, because you're going to send the invoice two weeks in advance, followed up by a friendly courtesy notice three days before it's due.

You've already gotten the point but I'll share one more anecdote because it's fun: I once worked with a designer who didn't enjoy calendarizing. We'll call her Antonia. She was gifted at designing the most amazing handbags I'd ever seen, but would rather spend her time shopping for houses online and complaining about the government. If she had 15 days to complete a project, this is how she'd use them:

- *Days 1 through 14: Shop online and read the news.*
- *Day 15: Go to the gym, go for a hike, Google a few things related to the project, complain about how the lead time for this project was way too short.*
- *Day 15, from 6 PM to 2 AM the next day: Do the project.*
- *Day 16: Deliver the project, one day late.*

We are not talking about an amateur here. Antonia had been designing handbags at the highest level for over a decade. And still, the above scenario would play out every time.

As you can imagine, starting to work on the very last day would be a disastrous approach to, say, a nine-month "footwear innovation" project. But if this happens during one short phase, it's less disastrous.

I began using a courtesy notice strategy on Antonia. Sometimes, I'd build in a little three-day cushion that Antonia didn't know about.

It pays to consistently remind yourself that the key to getting money seven days from now is finishing the project in that amount of time. Are we anxious about the deadline? Not sure how to manage our time? That's OK, the calendar tells us exactly what to do.

By now you might be thinking "OK, I get it, it's important to deliver on time. I'll just work fast and stay on track—and I can do that without a calendar."

No you can't. Make your calendar, set your alerts, and deliver early.

8.4 *Stay Organized: Systems, Tools, Apps*

> *"Watch out for intellect, because it knows so much it knows nothing."*
>
> — Anne Sexton

It's easy to organize a single project, but what about working on four client projects at the same time? It's tempting to always be on the hunt for the latest project management app, but unless you're an agency with 10+ employees, you can skip those. The best tool is one that you'll actually use—a very, very basic spreadsheet could do the trick. If you're like me, you want a zoomed-out overview that keeps you on top of the big picture. Something like this.[17]

Looks pretty rudimentary, huh? It is. I'll share a secret with you—for a freelance operation, complex tools and systems are mostly BS.

I'm currently operating an executive recruiting business with six open projects, editing this book and outlining the next one, planning two product drops, and making a business plan for next year. How do I stay on top of it all? Mostly, I use the apps that came with my phone. Calendar, Reminders, Mail, iChat. I wrote this book in Evernote and then I saved it in Dropbox.

I am a person of average intelligence, if that. I get overwhelmed easily. If I want to manage my self-imposed workload and have energy left over for friends, family, and hobbies, I must have a simple system for managing my time and energy. For me, it's leaving tomorrow's to-do list on my desk

---

17. https://www.dropbox.com/s/5ywoyojus2suf8m/Multiple%20client%20calendar.xlsx?dl=

at the end of each day, laying out my clothes, and having a cold brew waiting in the fridge right next to my desk. Why? So that at 6am, there are as few steps as possible between my sleepy ass and my goals.

Your routine might be the exact opposite of mine, and that's cool, as long as you have one.

Perhaps you have a high mental capacity for complexity, learning new apps, and constantly refining your process. Great, but I might suggest channeling that energy into your art. The more tricky systems you use, the more excuses you can give yourself for not getting the job done.

I'll wrap up with two key encouragements:

1. What seems overwhelming to you right now will be a breeze one year from now. It doesn't get easier, you just get better.
2. Writing down your priorities regularly (digitally, on paper, on a whiteboard, whatever) and looking at them is powerful. Just look at them. Maybe once a day. When I keep a tidy overview of my top priorities in my subconscious mind, I'm much less likely to get pulled into tangential minutiae.

Freelance success is about consistent behavior, not being smarter or more technologically advanced than everyone else.

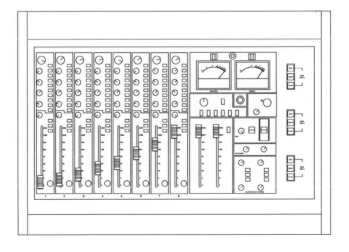

9 Get Your Money

"He who hesitates is lost."

— adapted from the play *Cato*, 1712

9.1 *Getting Paid On Time*

9.1.1 AGREEMENTS AND EXPECTATIONS

I once read an account of how Michael Phelps wins so many races. When he wakes up on race day, he does the same things he does every other day.

He eats, does his workout, sits in the sauna listening to a specific playlist on his headphones.

He comes out to the pool, does his warmup laps, puts his headphones back on, same playlist.

At some point near the end of this day-long routine, he dives into the pool and wins a swimming race.

For Phelps, a race is not some unique event that exists somewhere in the future and incites anxiety as it approaches. Rather, competing—and winning—are just the final dominos after all of the other dominos have fallen, like they always do. That playlist is just the playlist he listens to before he wins a race.

The same is true of you getting paid.

Getting paid on time is not the result of doing the work or sending the invoice. Getting paid on time is the result of something you did before any of that: you created an agreement with the client.

An *agreement* is the exact opposite of an *expectation*. Expectations are vague and unenforceable because they are based on assumptions. Assuming the client understands how bad you need the money. Assuming they have the same definition of "fair" as you do. Assuming they're cool with the payment terms listed in your fine print.

Clients, when they pay late, are usually just doing their job and adhering to the unspoken norm. Often in that world, it is perfectly acceptable to pay late because they know that all their vendors are accustomed to it and will likely take zero action when it happens.

It's not malicious; in fact, in many cases, business owners consider it best practice to defer all outgoing payments (not just yours, so this isn't personal) as long as possible and keep the highest possible amount of cash in the bank at all times. So they might avoid stating their Accounts Payable terms clearly, instead just assuming that everything will be ok when they pay at their own pace.

Understanding this, you must make an agreement with them before any work is done.

A big part of creating this agreement is simply asking for something and giving the client the power to say yes. It's like ordering popcorn at a movie theater. You're getting stale popcorn unless you ask for fresh popcorn. When you ask for fresh popcorn, you get it, 90% of the time, no questions asked. When this happens, you don't get mad at the fact that they were originally intending to give you stale popcorn. You understand that stale popcorn is their business model, you just hacked it, and they weren't even mad about it.

Since you've already had a fun, upbeat, and friendly conversation with your new client, expressing your respect for their brand and your gratitude for whatever mutual friend told them about you, creating this agreement should go smoothly.

That conversation might sound like:

You: "What are your payment terms?"

Them: "30 days."

You: "Got it. Mine are normally 15, but I can agree to 30 for the 2nd and 3rd invoices, if we can make an exception for invoice #1; I just need that one settled before the work starts."

Them: "Company policy prohibits me from authorizing any Net Zero payments, but I could do Net 15 for that first one."

You: "Thanks. If I can make that exception for the first invoice, could you agree to Net 15 for the rest of them as well?"

Them: "Sure, we can do that."

You: "Great. Much appreciated and I'll adjust the invoices accordingly. You'll have the first one in your inbox in a few minutes."

Make this agreement verbally in person or over the phone, follow it up with an email recap, and add to your invoices a note stating the date that the Net 15 agreement was made, and with whom.

9.1.2 **ENFORCEMENT**

When you make an *agreement* with your client, paying you late would mean they broke their own agreement. This rarely happens, because most humans like to keep their word. When you have an *expectation* that a client will read the due date on your invoice and act accordingly, you are most likely getting paid whenever their unspoken internal policy says it's convenient to pay you. Most likely a lot later than you were hoping. And as many wise people have said, hope is not a strategy.

There are only two things left to do:

1. Email your invoice on its "due date" (knowing that the agreed "payment date" is 15 days later).
2. Email a courtesy reminder three days before the "payment date," which is the actual due date based on Net 15.

If and when a client doesn't pay by the agreed date, the artist is no longer involved. It's time to bring in the enforcer. The enforcer is not an automated QuickBooks reminder that meekly asks them to "kindly remit."

The enforcer is your business manager, your bookkeeper, or maybe just you, making good use of the trust and personal report you have established with the client. And the message you are sending is that in order to keep the work flowing and the relationship in good standing, the outstanding amount needs to be settled by this very specific date.

The important thing here is that this message is not a surprise to your client. This isn't an ambush; this is a mutually expected event. If the enforcer's message is ignored, the work stops. If a client doesn't respond favorably to this, and you determine that they are now blatantly breaking a clear agreement they made with you, legal action is next. A letter from your lawyer will usually do the trick, because your contract backs you up. The downside here is that you'll never work with this client again, but that would have happened anyway, because this client did this to themselves.

In most cases, legal action won't be necessary. In most cases, you'll get your payment and the relationship will continue beautifully.

You might say, "Gee, thanks Michael for the tips on what I *should have* done, but I'm already in the middle of a difficult client scenario. I've submitted work and I'm owed money. What can I do *now*?" Great question.

A very talented and accomplished writer recently said to me: "I know writers who wait for literally years to get paid for work. They can't afford lawyers, and they don't want to burn bridges! These industries are small and everyone talks! My invoices say 'kindly send payment within 30 days of completion of the project.' What else can normal people do?"

Unfortunately, normal is absolutely the right word for this conundrum. If you have a client who is taking years to pay you, that particular bridge is already burning. Unless the client is in direct violation of an agreement by waiting years to pay, there's not much that *can* be done. You might call them and say, "Hey, looks like we've had an invoice outstanding for 24 months now. I realize we didn't have an agreement around payment terms; my mistake and I'll make sure to correct that next time. For now, can you let me know when we can expect to have this settled?" You can do this whether it's a small business owner or the intern in Accounts Payable at a giant corporation who finally answers your email—treat them like a person, and they might show up for you.

In lieu of any real leverage, this is just an appeal to their sense of fairness, which may or may not be effective. You might just have to let it go.

If we're talking about a quick two-day job with only one payment expected, and you've already turned over the work and don't have any leverage left, then your leverage becomes the next job. You delivered great work, on time, and they're going to want more of this. When they do, before you accept, call them and explain that due to the unfortunate outcome of the last project, you'll have to make different arrangements for this one.

This call *could* be intimidating and awkward, but it's not, because you're a professional. You have conducted yourself well, you use a nice tone of voice, and you separate the person from the problem.

It's not "You tried to rip me off last time, Sharon!"

It's "I understand that those circumstances were likely out of your control and mine, so I'll just need to collect payment up front this time. I'll be ready to dive in as soon as payment clears."

Here's a visual example of what your invoice should include:

EASY ON THE EXTRAS

Easy on the
Extras, Inc.
1234 Main Street
Los Angeles, CA 12345

INVOICE #:
ABC123 (#1 of 3)
January 7th, 2021

BANK DETAILS:
Account 12345678
Routing 12345678
SWIFT 12345678
Bill.com PNI: 12345678

CLIENT:
FICTIONAL NAME, INC
ATTN: Gertrude Smith, Accounts Payable
c/o Trip Fontaine, Project Manager
1234 Maple Street
New York, NY 12345

PROJECT:
FOOTWEAR DESIGN 1

SERVICES:

CONCEPT
Create direction brief based on client mood board

SKETCHING
Perform a maxiumum of two rounds of revisions
Create basic drawings to convey design intent

TECH PACKS
Perform a maximum of two rounds of revisions
Create tech packs based on client's approval of sketches
Include all necessary information for factory

INVOICE SUMMARY:

Project Total	~~$31,500.00~~
15% Friends / Family reduction	**$26,775.00**
Rush fees	$0.00
#1 Deposit due upon start of work	**$8,925.00**
#2 Due at or before meeting #2 - sketch handoff	$8,925.00
#3 Balance due upon delivery of final assets	$8,925.00

TOTAL DUE UPON RECIEPT   **$8,925.00**

PAYMENT IS DUE WITHIN 15 DAYS OF INVOICE DATE. LATE PAYMENT WILL INCUR A 3% MONTHLY PENALTY
ON OUTSTANDING BALANCE. PLEASE MAKE CHECKS OR WIRES PAYABLE TO: EASY ON THE EXTRAS, INC

Important things to note about this example, and incorporate into your own invoices:

1. It's not too difficult to look at. Use a format and font that leave plenty of white space. Tie it aesthetically to your brand, and to the proposal that got you here.

2. The services are listed, same as on the proposal, and the project name is included. No confusion about what this invoice is for.

3. Even though this is just the first invoice of three, all three invoice amounts are outlined. This way, anyone who wasn't involved in the money conversation still has a clear picture of the total amount owed, and knows that there will be two more invoices coming.

4. Even though you've made reference to three invoices total, you've clearly highlighted the specific amount due for this particular invoice (use whatever combination of font size and boldness you choose, and keep it classy).

5. It includes the name of the person in Accounts Payable who is directly responsible for payment, *and* the name of the project contact who approved this whole thing to begin with. If any internal confusion arises, these two people can find each other and speak directly.

6. All bank details are listed: account number, routing number, SWIFT code, Bill.com PNI (Payment Network ID), and even your mailing address. Give them every possible (reasonable) way to pay you, and zero reasons to delay.

7. The terms are at the bottom in the same size font as everything else. It's not screaming but it's not whispering either. Speak softly and carry a big stick.

9.2 *Forming an Entity*

> *"The mind is for having ideas, not holding them."*
>
> — David Allen

At some point in your freelance career, you're going to ask yourself this question: should I start a business?

When it comes to what people call your business and how the IRS will treat it, you have a few options. If you don't have any partners, you'll likely be choosing between an S Corporation, an LLC, or a sole proprietorship. A sole proprietorship is just you asking your clients to write checks to you personally (or your parents' bank account). This is sometimes also called a DBA, meaning you're an individual Doing Business As some registered business name.[18]

---

18. If you want to form a startup that may someday be a big corporation, you'd start a C Corporation, which is more complex and costly, and I won't cover it here.

The factors to consider when choosing how to proceed: your tax burden, your liability, and your overall professionalism. I'm not a tax professional, but I have a brilliant one on retainer, and she[19] helped me write this next part.

In my view, if your freelance work isn't just a passing phase and you plan to make a real go of it, it almost always makes sense to form a business entity. The reasons for doing so have shifted with the tax law (and probably always will, so stay in touch with your CPA), but if you can afford the few hundred dollars it costs to form a business entity, and the subsequent tax ($800 per year in LLC tax or 1.5% tax on net income for your S Corporation), the tax savings will likely more than make up for it. Why? Because businesses are generally taxed at a lower rate than people are.

Here's a tidy breakdown of what forming and maintaining the two most common entity types (LLC or S Corp) will cost you on an annual basis (picking California, one of the higher-tax states, as an example):

- **One-time costs**

  - Formation: $500–$1,500

- **Annual costs**

  - California Tax: $800–1.5% of net income
  - California LLC fee (gross revenues $250,000–$499,999; doesn't apply to S Corps): $900
  - Tax Services (CPA): $500–$2,500
  - Annual (or Bi-Annual) Statement of Information filing fee: $20–$25
  - Bookkeeping software (yes, you need this): $300–$840
  - Bookkeeping service (yes, you need this): $2,400–$7,800
  - City Business License: $1.01–$4.50 per $1,000 of gross revenues
  - Payroll processing (only applies to S Corps): $540

So it costs roughly $5,000 annually in taxes and professional service fees to run your business entity. (Actually less than that, because even if you don't form an entity, you're still required to keep your books and file your taxes). Sounds like a lot, but remember, *all of those costs are tax-deductible* and a good CPA is trained to help you identify all the ways to offset (or more than offset) those costs.

---

19. https://www.cpacollective.com/about

Nuance applies to all of the above, so call your CPA—or go hire one now!—to see what's right for you. My CPA actually wanted to go into more detail here in this book, but I wouldn't let her, because your eyes would glaze over. If your questions go beyond what this book offers, you should be seeking the advice of a money professional. If you have no idea where to start, a free consultation is pretty standard. Free personalized professional knowledge is as good as free money, so take advantage.

If these costs are a deterrent for you because you aren't currently pulling in that much money, let's work on changing that. The moment you can reasonably project that you'll earn enough (and deduct enough) to offset that rough $5K figure I mentioned above, form your entity. If you're quibbling internally about whether you're going to make $63K or $68K next year, you're thinking about this wrong. Instead, plot a path to $150K (or some number that feels the right combination of thrilling, scary, and feasible) and build your entity accordingly. You plan to grow, right? No reason to delay this.

Aside from the financial reasons to form an entity, here are two more:

1. **Legal protection.** Put bluntly, we live in a litigious society and you can get sued for almost any reason. If this happens, it's good to have a layer of paperwork between your business and you. The importance of that layer will depend on your art. Craftspeople who build barstools might be more likely to get sued than graphic designers. Maybe.[20]

2. **Professionalism.** You want to attract money from clients. Businesses want to send electronic payments to other businesses, not send a Venmo to someone's cousin.

You've spoken to your CPA to determine what type of entity is best for you, and what it will cost—a good lawyer can handle the rest. Personally, I use CPA Collective[21] for all tax advice (they specialize in small businesses and freelancers) and Better[22] for my entity formation needs, but there are many options for both. For more legal protection, may also want to consider liability insurance, especially if you're a sole proprietor. State laws vary, but a few Google searches will or a recommendation from your CPA will set you straight.

---

20. https://www.unifiedmanufacturing.com/blog/design-copyright-infringement-costly-cases/

21. https://www.cpacollective.com/

22. https://inbetterwetrust.com/

Recap: if you can afford to formalize your business as an entity, do it now. If you can't afford it now, use this book to get yourself to a place where you can. If you have no intention of growing your business to a size that would necessitate the bare minimum outlined above, then I love you but this isn't the book for you.

9.3 *Banking, Collecting, and Saving*

> *"We live in a fantasy world, a world of illusion. The great task in life is to find reality."*
>
> — Iris Murdoch

Once your entity is formed, you can take that paperwork to your bank of choice and open a business account. Put your new account number, routing number, SWIFT code, and bank branch address on your invoices. Now your clients can send electronic payments.

One hack I discovered years ago via Ramit Sethi's[23] book is that many banks will allow you to open multiple savings accounts, nickname them, and link them together. As a person, this helps you save for different goals—car, wedding, vacation, house. As a freelancer, this helps you organize your income, most importantly by setting aside for taxes.

Here's how I do it:

When a payment comes in, immediately send 35% of it to a savings account named "Taxes." Why 35%? It's a bit arbitrary, but the main reason is that it roughly represents the maximum you are likely to need come tax season. If this is imprecise, or even overkill, fine. At the end of the year, a surplus is better than a shortfall.

Do that every month, amassing a tidy pile of money that is reserved for the IRS. Maybe.

Your CPA will help you create and pay quarterly tax estimates, or wait until December to pay it all at once, depending on what type of entity you form.

If all goes well, your deductions could reduce your tax bill, meaning you might not owe the full amount you've saved. Examples of deductions:

- Your office space or a portion of your rent if you work from home
- Your equipment

---

23. https://www.amazon.com/Will-Teach-You-Rich-Second/dp/1523505745

- The things you purchase as reference samples or learning materials
- Meals or coffees you buy for clients
- Potentially many other things which your CPA will help you identify

If this happens and you have money left over, you can contribute the difference to your SEP IRA (imagine a 401(k), but without the part where your employer chooses non-optimal funds on your behalf and passes the excessive management fees onto you), reducing your tax bill even more, and also making you rich over time. It's like a wonderful circular turbocharger of wealth building. I'll write a separate book on the topic. For now, just open a business bank account and follow those three steps.

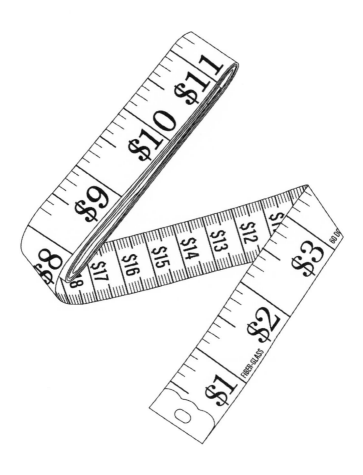

10 Client Relationships

"The line separating good and evil runs... right through every human heart."

— Aleksandr I. Solzhenitsyn

Let's address the fallacy of the Bad Client. Many creative people believe that there are good clients and bad clients, and all you have to do is avoid the bad ones, and the good ones will just be totally cool to you without you having to require it.

This, of course, is false.

You're probably super good at being creative. Great. That's a start, but it won't ensure that you're treated fairly or compensated according to your talent.

The world is not full of good guys and bad guys, but just people who mostly don't know what they're doing. It's your job to help your clients figure it out, by being organized, laying out what you're going to do and what it will cost, how you expect to be paid, and by being trustworthy yourself. 50% of every client relationship is 100% you.

Are there bad clients? Yes. Like the one we fired back at the start of this book, they are out there. But as I learned the hard way, in most cases your client will be as good as your ability to properly set up the relationship. Everyone has the potential for evil. It's up to you to bring out the best in people.

You don't get what you deserve; you get what you tolerate.

10.1 *The Happy Client*

Top four reasons you should do what it takes to absolutely delight every client you work with:

1. It's the right thing to do and it makes life more enjoyable.
2. They'll hire you again. It's more efficient to gain repeat clients than to go find new clients. Both are good of course, but in some professions, six really great clients could be all you need from now until you retire. Do the math on how wonderful your business could look if every client

you have now would happily hire you three times per year, in perpetu-
ity.

3. They'll refer you to other clients. Those clients could also become
   repeat clients. Now we're talking about compound growth.
4. The more happy clients you have, the more agency you have. You can
   decide to work with great people rather than be forced to take whatever
   you can get.

Remember, your client is professional (and if they aren't, still, treat
them like they are) and they are either A) accustomed to dealing with professionals or B) not accustomed to dealing with professionals and will be
pleasantly surprised when dealing with you.

If you're a people person, client relationships are fun. If you're not a
people person, client relationships are a fun challenge.

Find something in common with your contact at the company, and
show interest in them. Be their friend, send them links to articles they will
enjoy, introduce them to great people, add value to their lives, and have
fun with it.

Look them in the eye and speak without filler words and most importantly, when you get the job, crush it. Over-deliver, and over-deliver early.

Make certain that you are the best, easiest to deal with, funniest, most
complimentary and pleasant professional they've ever hired.

Now you've got a long-term client, which means you're busier than you
were yesterday. The thing about busy people is their value goes up.

Once you have elevated a client to "long term" status, here a few suggestions for maintaining that relationship:

- **If it's sensitive, pick up the phone.** Texts and emails are great for
  saying "Hi" and answering basic questions, but terrible for important
  or nuanced conversations. These include negotiations, taking feedback or criticism that could be misconstrued, or anything that needs
  to remain confidential. A good rule of thumb for anything you're con-
  sidering putting in writing: assume it will be A) misunderstood and B)
  forwarded.
- **Touch base between jobs.** I don't mean, "Hey, it's been a while, got
  any work for me?" but rather, "Check out this article, it reminds me of
  our last conversation. Hope you're well!"

- **Send Thanksgiving gifts.** It's unexpected (nobody sends gifts on Thanksgiving), it's sincere (attach a note expressing how grateful you are for their partnership), and it's classy (make it all about them, not you).

10.2 *When to Fire a Client*

> *"A person is constituted in language. As such, when a person's word is less than whole and complete, they are diminished as a person."*
>
> — Michael Jensen

◇ IMPORTANT Not being able to fire a deadbeat client, and thus being locked into a toxic relationship for money reasons, defeats the whole purpose of freelancing.

Many, if not most, of your client frustrations might stem from the fact that you can't leave the clients you have, because you don't have any new ones coming in.

The best time to fire a client is when you have another one. This was a realization I had with the client from Chapter 1. Why was there so much stress involved with this one client who wouldn't pay us? Why were we even working for such a client anyway? We were forced to. Because at that time, we had nothing else going on.

In an ideal world, with a full client roster, or maybe even a waiting list, we could have politely asked that client to buzz off the moment they showed the first sign of dishonesty.

"We understand you're having cash flow problems. We can of course be flexible but we can't work for free without a plan. Let us know how much time you need, and until then we'll pause the work and ramp back up when we have a solution in place."

But we couldn't say that, because we didn't have any other clients. If you're in a position like we were, ignore what we discussed in Price Your Work,[§6] and just go get some clients.

Do discounted work, do free work, give gifts, get your work into places where people will see it, be generous, and get people talking about you. Once you have built a community of people and companies who are happy to trade you money for your work, you have earned the ability to activate the strategies outlined in chapters 4 and 5.

In the rare case that you do encounter a bad client, and you've taken all personal and professional steps to foster a good relationship to no avail, cut them loose. One of the best privileges of a freelancer is the privilege to fire a client.

When you're certain it has to be done, do it. Do it kindly and professionally:

- *Never* in writing (amateur move), always verbally (ideally over the phone). This is hard, but do it anyway. You want to leave zero room for interpretation, and let them hear your sincere tone of voice.
- Leave anger and frustration out of it: "I've had a lot of fun working with you guys but it has become apparent that we are not the right fit for each other. I'm going to wrap up what I'm working on and then let you move on to someone else who can suit your needs. I wish you all the best."

⚠ CAUTION If you've made every possible effort outlined in this book to develop a good relationship with the client, and there's still a significant amount of money outstanding, then call a lawyer before you have the above conversation. Depending on what type of written agreement you had (or didn't have) with the client, your lawyer can walk you through your options for collecting.

Taking this step will of course ensure that you never work with this client again, so be certain before you enter this territory. But once you decide, get it done quickly.

And then let it go, learn from it, and move on.

> *"Holding a grudge is a symptom of not knowing how you want to spend the gift of the day."*
>
> — Mike Maples, Jr.

11 Growing

"Be as you wish to seem."

— Socrates

11.1 *Be as You Wish to Seem*

I once coached a very talented Italian furniture designer. We'll call her Chianti. Her portfolio is full of work for Zaha Hadid and other beautiful designs for prestigious clients.

If you or I would have glanced at Chianti's portfolio or met her in person, we would have seen a successful, stylish, talented professional who would undoubtedly command high rates for her work. Large, high-revenue clients look at her work and see it in the same way.

The trouble was, Chianti had a different image of herself. When a client approached her, she assumed they were just looking for the cheapest option, so she became that option. When I encouraged her to aim higher, she said she was afraid to lose the job by being too expensive.

Here's the thing though: she *is* expensive.

Her designs and products are expensive, her taste is expensive, her whole vibe is expensive. Her private clients have money, otherwise they wouldn't be able to afford her dining tables for their homes. Her corporate clients were the same way—looking for quality, ready to pay.

But there was a disconnect.

- **The client:** Accustomed to success, money to spend, approaching the designer, looking to upgrade their office space with a luxurious new interior design. Abundance mentality.
- **The designer herself:** Needing the work, thinking of paying her rent, assuming the client was in the same boat—and she let her self-doubt leak into the conversation. Scarcity mentality.

When I noticed this dynamic, I realized we needed to reset the playing field. We rebuilt Chianti's proposal, upped her price, and changed the overall tone. The client responded by nonchalantly paying the full asking price, without so much as a discussion.

Chianti was ecstatic. All I did was point out what was obvious to me but obscured for her: what her art was worth.

I had a similar experience with a very high caliber digital design studio. Their portfolio consisted of amazing marketing work for huge name brands, with impressive results.

But when they sat down with me to get my advice on how to grow, their language consisted of things like, "We're still paying our dues as a studio," and, "We're having a hard time getting our normal rate so we've been discounting a lot of work recently."

Bro I just saw your portfolio. It's 75 pages long and full of impeccable work for household names! You drove here in a Land Rover and you're wearing a $3,000 leather jacket. Your accessories don't necessarily *equal* success, but they signal it. Your prospective clients know that. Do *you* know that?

Lots of freelancers tend to be self-deprecating because they associate confidence with being a jerk. This is false. You are not Ari Gold, you are a talented creative who delivers great work to clients who love you.

It's very important to integrate your past successes into your professional identity. If you did a photo shoot for Budweiser, you are now a photographer who has worked with Budweiser. Will every client have a Budweiser-sized budget? No, but they want to work with the photographer who did the Budweiser campaign they've seen on all the billboards, and they'll expect it to cost money.

Please make sure that you give yourself credit for how capable and accomplished you are. In doing so, please also understand that confidence and humility are not mutually exclusive. In fact, they are a powerful duo.

When you combine a high level of self-respect *with a smile* and some manners and a personal touch, the result is the ability to calmly say things that might otherwise feel uncomfortable. You can now stand up for yourself and create boundaries. Some more examples:

- *(smile)* "Just a heads up; it looks like our delivery date is being pushed out three days, because I received the assets three days late. No problem, I'm already on it — and I'll see if we can make it two days." *(smile)*
- *(smile)* "I'd love to work with you but I've got a certain capacity and a very full plate, so I'm a bit limited in my ability to discount my work at the moment. But let's talk about scope; maybe we can make this happen." *(smile)*

- *(smile)* "My standard turnaround time is five business days but it looks like you need them tomorrow. I've included the rush fee in the proposal." *(smile)*

Understand the professional plane on which you seek to exist. Visualize what a successful freelance business looks like, and who a successful freelancer is. Then be that person. Take the actions that a successful freelancer would take, and see what happens.

The correct order is Zig Ziglar's: "Be, Do, Have."

11.2 *Network Like Hell*

> "*It's not enough to be nice in life. You've got to have nerve.*"
>
> — Georgia O'Keeffe

Freelance success is as much about how you deal with people as it is any artistic talent you possess.

You've built an exceptional business and you want people to know about it. You want to command larger amounts of money, you want to diffuse conflict, you want to calm people, you want them to trust you. Not all clients (or potential clients) are going to be easy to talk to. But you can win them over anyway, with thoughtfulness, as well as your voice and your body language.

George J. Thompson, author of *Verbal Judo,* wrote: "On the phone, where your ONVs (Other Non-Verbals) can't come into play, content remains at 7 to 10 percent of your impact, while voice makes up the rest. Think about that. The goods, the truth, the point in these encounters is almost irrelevant compared to your voice and body language (ONVs)! The facts don't speak for themselves in court, in an arrest situation, in your office, or at home. People aren't buying what you say; they're concentrating on how you're saying it."

Entire books have been written about voice and body language, and I'm no expert. But I know a hack: have fun.

Self-awareness creates awkwardness. The more fun you're having, the less self aware you are, and the more favorably you come across.

I used to be afraid of dealing with new people. I only dealt with people who made it easy for me to deal with them. People who dressed like I did, liked the cars I liked, or made the first conversational move.

Later, I learned that relating to un-relatable people is a fun skill to master. I started to challenge myself to make friends with the most unlikely person in the room. When I was a dirtbag BMX rider I made friends with a doctor, and then a Senior VP at a fashion brand. When I was a hip fashion dude I made friends with real estate developers and food and wine experts. Later, entrepreneurs and CEOs. I focused on people outside of my comfort zone and demographic.

I started to notice a pattern of great consulting work coming my way approximately six months after I made a new friend.

Networking is important, but that's not why you should do it. Do it because it's fun.

One reason many creative people despise networking is because they place a strong delineation between friends and clients. They view friends as the people they want to spend time with, while clients are a necessary evil, existing far away from your sphere; strange aliens with money that you want to extract without getting too close.

I know a graphic designer who hangs out exclusively with people who make art, wear all black and look exactly like him. It's a wonderful group of creative people with big hearts, a strong sense of loyalty to each other, and very low incomes. By existing in such an isolated space, they have no idea how to relate to their clients (except for when their clients are hip dive bars in need of new signage). That communication gap leads to some pretty frustrating—or in the best case, unsatisfying—projects. Add up the hours of each day that people like this spend working for clients that they can't relate to, complaining about them while at the same time needing more of them— that's a big chunk of life that is unenjoyable.

I nominate you to not be that way.

This is the mindset adjustment that needs to happen: view making friends and getting clients as virtually the same thing.

As a successful small business, your first customers are usually your friends, and that's not awkward unless you make it so. When you care enough to deliver excellence to your friends, your friends tell other people and pretty soon your client list extends far beyond that circle. This is a much better approach than waiting for a client who has never heard of you to notice your work.

For quieter people like me, matters of taste are a great way to create new relationships. Compliment someone's shoes, call out something specific about their photography on Instagram, ask about their obscure vintage handbag. A question that only a person of a particular taste would know how to ask.

A personal example: I'm obsessed with cars. I used to spend my free time researching them, shopping for them, driving them, talking about them—never imagining that the large group of acquaintances that I was inadvertently amassing would grow to become a big portion of my social group. It just happened.

Some of us organized an annual vintage car rally together. Soon 40 people were in attendance. They became friends too. Then some of those friends became business partners, some became clients, some became trusted contacts who referred me to clients without me asking them to.

Think about this in your specific context. Maybe you're a UX designer. If you were to build a group of 40–80 new acquaintances with the same hobby as you, there's a good chance that a large percentage of them (or *their* friends) will need a UX designer in their life. And when that need arises, they're not going to do a LinkedIn search—they're going to call the person they know and like (that's you).

Once you have developed the muscle for amassing friends with shared hobbies, you can then easily and confidently approach (or be approached by) other professionals who have the ability to hire you, whether they share your hobby or not.

In summary, friends are people who enjoy you, believe in you, and trust you. Substitute the word "clients" for "friends" and that sentence is still just as true. So don't be afraid to mix it up. Here's a quick set of guidelines to get you started:

Don't:

- Pay money for a seminar or networking events
- Overthink it
- Transactionalize it

Do:

- Reach out to people of similar tastes and values
- Make a mental list of the top three things you do that your friends love about you
- Do those things for more people

11.3 *Build Your Team*

> *"I will not reason and compare; my business is to create."*
> — William Blake

The purpose of this book has been to nudge you into a transition from talented creative to successful freelancer. Your confidence and finesse now match the level of your creative skills. You are cash flow positive and you're not afraid of the future.

This is a nice place to be. Where you go next is completely up to you. The "be your own boss" spectrum is a big one: it ranges from one person cranking out goods and services to, well, Jeff Bezos I guess. Choosing where you'd like to sit on that spectrum (and changing your mind as often as you'd like) is a right that you've granted yourself.

Back in 2018, Jeff Staple interviewed the designer and musician Hiroshi Fujiwara[24] about his life and career. In that interview Hiroshi revealed some fascinating stuff. One example: Hiroshi is actually unaware of his net worth. He wants to create, collaborate, and collect the design objects he's passionate about, and that's it. If he's, say, attending an auction and ready to place a $175K bid on a rare timepiece, he calls his business manager and asks if he can afford it. He gets a yes or no answer and proceeds accordingly.

Hiroshi has earned the ability to not concern himself with money. He can expand his company, fragment design, into a giant agency. Or not. In the introduction to the Fujiwara interview, Staple writes, "How many people does it take to run a successful company? Well, according to fragment design founder Hiroshi Fujiwara, the answer is just three. But a dizzying network of friends and connections to myriad industries help, too."

Three takeaways here:

1. The purpose of upping your freelance game is to assert more control over your own life. With money in the bank you can sleep deeply at night and spend your time how you want, with whom you want.
2. If Hiroshi can operate a studio as productive and influential as fragment design with only two employees, what might be possible for you?
3. However large or small you decide to make your team, I recommend that you espouse the "we" mentality.

---

24. https://hypebeast.com/2018/2/
business-of-hype-jeff-staple-01-hiroshi-fujiwara-fragment-design

Even if your employee count is zero, your "team" is generally comprised of four groups:

- **Group 1:** The bookkeeper, CPA, and lawyer that we know you will inevitably need.
- **Group 2:** Designers. Websites, presentations, and brand identities all need professional attention and unless that professional is you, then you need these people at your fingertips.
- **Group 3:** Assistants. You might need a virtual assistant in India. You might need an IRL assistant, three hours per week. You might need a team of runners crisscrossing town making pickups and deliveries. I used to use TaskRabbit until I came across a couple of dependable people that I'm happy to just text when I need them.

These first three groups of people can be contracted on an as-needed basis to keep your payroll and fixed costs at an absolute minimum. The fourth group is free.

- **Group 4:** Your personal BOD (board of directors).

Some of them might be mentors; some might just be peers whose opinions you trust because lives they've built are reflections of good decision making. The single best move you can make as a professional freelancer is to improve the quality of your inner circle—don't be afraid to punch above your weight class. If you follow the steps outlined in Network Like Hell,[§11.2] these types of people will start appearing in your life.

If you want to be effective without being exhausted and miserable, you need good people around you. Like Hiroshi demonstrates, it's possible to have heavy hitters at your disposal without being responsible for an excess of employees. Many wise people have said "outsource everything but your genius." Your genius is your art.

11.4 *The Last Word*

> *"Success is not to be pursued; it is to be attracted by the person*
> *you become."*
>
> — Jim Rohn

I suspect that I haven't told you anything new in these chapters. If you're anything like the former me, you were intuitively aware that a certain amount of professionalism, process knowledge, and awareness of human nature are vital to making money as a freelancer.

For me, the surprise was not that these things were necessary; it was that they can be learned. They're not inherent skills that one must be born with. I certainly wasn't.

Now that you know this, what are you capable of?

12 Reading List

"Art has its own rules. And one of them is that you must pay more attention to it than anything else in the world, if you don't, and you are an artist, it punishes you."

— Nina Simone

- *The Psychology of Money,*[25] by Morgan Housel
- *Illuminate,*[26] by Nancy Duarte and Patti Sanchez
- *Verbal Judo,*[27] George J. Thompson and Jerry B. Jenkins
- *The Magic of Thinking Big,*[28] by David J. Schwartz
- *High Performance Habits,*[29] by Brendon Burchard
- *Shorter,*[30] by Alex Soojung-Kim Pang
- *Willpower Doesn't Work,*[31] by Ben Hardy
- *The War of Art,*[32] by Steven Pressfield
- *The Laws of Human Nature,*[33] by Robert Greene
- *Never Split the Difference,*[34] by Chris Voss
- *Distinguishing Between Hobbies, Jobs, Careers, and Vocation*[35] (Acumen Academy), a wonderful and relevant talk by Elizabeth Gilbert.

25. https://www.amazon.com/Psychology-Money-Timeless-lessons-happiness/dp/0857197681
26. https://www.amazon.com/Illuminate-Through-Speeches-Stories-Ceremonies/dp/1101980168
27. https://www.amazon.com/Verbal-Judo-Gentle-Persuasion-Updated/dp/0062107704
28. https://www.amazon.com/Magic-Thinking-Big-David-Schwartz/dp/0671646788
29. https://www.amazon.com/High-Performance-Habits-Extraordinary-People/dp/1401952852
30. https://www.amazon.com/Shorter-Work-Better-Smarter-Heres/dp/1541730712
31. https://www.amazon.com/Willpower-Doesnt-Work-Discover-Success/dp/0316441325
32. https://www.amazon.com/The-War-of-Art-Steven-Pressfield-audiobook/dp/B07PTBYH2G
33. https://www.amazon.com/Laws-Human-Nature-Robert-Greene/dp/0525428143
34. https://www.amazon.com/Never-Split-Difference-audiobook/dp/B01COR1GM2
35. https://www.youtube.com/watch?v=0g7ARarFNnw

About the Author

Michael Ardelean has always worked at the intersection of art and money. Having grown up bored and broke in suburban Detroit, Michael knew how to get a lot out of a little—streamlining processes and shaking off the baggage of life is his guiding philosophy. His first career, as a pro BMX biker, inspired him to share this outlook and his strategies with others struggling to design a comfortable life around their passion. He moved into merchandising, with a VP role at Alternative Apparel, followed by several years managing a design studio. Michael then began helping creative freelancers with the business end of their work as a consultant. Today, he runs his own recruiting firm, Intro, with the goal of improving organizations (like Madhappy and Buck Mason) by empowering individuals. His passion is advocating for artists of all kinds by helping them make their unique talents financially viable. Michael's new book, Art For Money, shows creative freelancers what can happen when you cut out what's not serving you, focus on what you can improve, and dream big.

About Holloway

Holloway publishes books online, offering titles from experts on topics ranging from tools and technology to teamwork and entrepreneurship. All titles are built for a satisfying reading experience on the web as well as in print. The Holloway Reader helps readers find what they need in search results, and permits authors and editors to make ongoing improvements.

Holloway seeks to publish more exceptional authors. We believe that a new company with modern tools can make publishing a better experience for authors and help them reach their audience. If you're a writer with a manuscript or idea, please get in touch at hello@holloway.com.